THA1

"[C]ompelling, and easily the best book I have read in quite some time. This book needs to be in all hands."

–Susan Conway, Author of A LIFE OF WHOREDOM

"Jeff has a raw and unapologetic approach to life and the many quirks and hiccups that challenge our everyday journey towards the grave."

–Jonas Jorselje, Five-Star Amazon Review

"It was delivered today and I devoured it as soon I opened the package."

–B. Budny, Five-Star Amazon Review

"This book of 'poetry' is horrible. I read the whole thing, and will buy the next one."

–JL, Five-Star Amazon Review

"Most poets are dreamy and tell all the words you want to hear. False hopes and fantasies. [Welch] tells it how it is and it resonates to the core for those of us that can relate."

–Tabitha Clark, Five-Star Amazon Review

ALSO BY J. WARREN WELCH

Your Mom Thinks It's Poetry

"Caroline"
a short horror story featured in
Witches of the Wood

That's Not
POETRY

J. WARREN WELCH

BIG SMALL TOWN BOOKS

Published by Big Small Town Books,
an imprint of Big Small Town Entertainment.

www.bigsmalltownbooks.com

Formal requests to the publisher may be sent to:

Big Small Town Books
P.O. Box 311
Unicoi, Tennessee, 37692

Reviewers may quote brief passage as part of their reviews.

Paperback ISBN 978-1-07-062747-2 • Also available as an eBook.

Cover Designed and Copyright © 2019 Dustin Street. Images courtesy of Pixabay and @j.warren.welch Instagram.

Printed in the United States of America. This book utilizes the Avenir family of fonts, as well as Iowan Old Style Roman and Tox Typewriter typefaces.

11 10 9 8 7 6 5 4 3   20 21 22 23 24 25 26

First published in January, 2018 by The Casual Word Publishing.

For Natasha.

There's no way this would have happened without you, baby. Thank you for loving me in a way that makes me feel like it's okay to be the person I've always known that I am, and for being the kind of woman I will never think I deserve to get to share my life with.

I really hope this is just the beginning of my artistic endeavors, and perhaps one day I will be able to give you everything you truly deserve in life. You are my best friend, in a way that has forced me to redefine the depths of what that term means.

I love your fucking face, bitch, and I always will.

CONTENTS

That's Not
POETRY

"That's Not Poetry."

Did I ask you, motherfucker?

FOREWORD

There are writers and then there is Jeff Welch. In a world filled with a bevy of poets vying for their spot in this new age of "social media art," he simply *is*. There are few, if any, as unpretentious, as genuine, and as unique, and to say he's a breath of fresh air is quite the understatement. Jeff holds nothing back in life and it shows in his words. He's not afraid to defend the underdog at the drop of a hat, proclaim his love for his wife with a visceral and unabashed passion, welcome his imperfections with open arms whilst sharing them openly, and, most importantly, he remains steadfast in his aim to uplift us all. As far as writers go, Jeff's inimitable way with words is worth noting. The words that follow are sure to make you laugh, look within, and keep you on your toes.

–Sarah Murdock
@sarahmariawrites

We can be monsters
You and I
Just like everyone else
But without the disguise

It could never be enough
I will never be done
There will be no moment
When my lips have had their fill of yours
It is the kind of thirst
That can never possibly be quenched
Always
Every moment
My entire soul screams
Just
One
More

On Sunday
We worship
Each other

We were both too exhausted

From long roads

To hide who we really were any longer

We were both too weary

From long years

To try to be anything other than ourselves

We had no strength

For effort

Left

Then we found each other

And we were home

And it was easy

And now...

We can rest

There's just something about

The way she stands

Her posture

Shoulders back

Chin up

Back arched

So fucking sexy

I've not looked at her one single time

Without my mind instantly fantasizing

About all the unholy things I want to do with her
    naked body...

But it's so much more than just

Intoxicating primal lust

When she stands like that

I really believe she might just take over the world

The whole fucking world

And when she does

I want to be right there beside her

No man

Has ever needed

Supervision

As much as I do

And no woman

Has ever made

Being supervised

Feel as much like freedom

As she does

You know that warm feeling
In your gut
That makes you hard
And makes you wet?
You think that's love
Don't you?
That's not love
That's just biology's way
Of making biological shit
Seem a lot more fun
Love is even more primal than that
It is a moment-to-moment
Fight-or-flight decision
Love is found in those moments
When the hair on your neck stands up
And you bare your teeth
And protect each other's necks
Love is when you know that
Good or bad
Day or night
Win or lose
Live or die...
This is your fucking person
And you're going to face everything
Together

It was just a moment
Both of us on our way
From different point As
To different point Bs
Just a moment
With you in my arms
And your lips pressed to mine
And it made the entire day
Beautiful

Let's just be
Damaged
Together

I don't call her
"Darling"
When I write about her
Because in real life I say
"I love you, bitch"
And she says
"I love you, motherfucker"
And we both get those
Silly little butterflies in our stomach
That's the kind of love
I've always wanted

It never feels
Freaky or filthy
When we do all those
Wonderful things
We do to each other
It just feels like
Making love

It's almost as if
The moment we found each other
Some sort of Karmic balance
Was thrown violently off its axis
And ever since that instant
Not one single thing
Has gone right for us
That's okay
The universe can do
Whatever it needs to do
To reset its equilibrium
And when the dust settles
We'll be standing right here together
Exhausted from laughter
And amazing sex
With four middle fingers in the air

Poets write
Intense lines like
"I would die for you"
And then that passion
Unbacked by resolve
Disappears
As soon as the ink runs out
But you and I both know
I'm not really a poet

Being loved by you
Makes every breath
Feel less like a chore
And more
Like a miracle

She still has these
Little moments of anxiety
When she thinks
She doesn't "deserve" me
And she's scared she might lose me
She doesn't understand
That I was never a man worth having
Until she gave me the freedom
To be myself
And there is no fucking way
That I will ever let that go

And I still
Wake up
Wanting
You

If it takes more than just one lifetime
And more words than I can write
If it takes more hugs than my arms can handle
And more kisses than my lips can take
If we have to make love even more than
My insatiable appetite can fathom
I will make her understand
How deep
And unconditional
My love for her really is
And more importantly
She will know that she deserves
Far more than that
And that I am the one
Who won the lottery
When we found each other

I would rather live
One difficult life
With you
Than a thousand easy lives
Without you

We are perfect for each other

Exactly how we are

But that does not mean

That we should not change

Together

And grow

Together

Conquer demons and vices

Together

Get

Better

Together

And become even more

Perfect for each other

Together

I really don't believe
We will ever run out of
Wonderful new things
To do to each other

Every fairy tale has its midnight
That moment when the clock strikes twelve
And the brutality of real life turns your beautiful
    fantasies upside down
At that point
It takes more guts than butterflies
And more balls than cock
To carry on
And this is where most people give up
But I'm not most people
I am equal parts lover and fighter
And as good as I am at the fairy tale
I'm probably even better suited for those terrifying
    midnight battles
Our clock struck twelve long ago
And now it seems like the top of every hour
Is another fucking midnight
But this is still our goddamn fairy tale
The kind of love story where two lovers
Survive against every conceivable foe
And emerge at the end covered in blood and
    sweat
But still holding tightly to each other
And those are my favorite kind of love stories
    anyway

When the light
Hits your face
Just right...
The light
Becomes more beautiful

At my last moment

In that small space

Between right now

And forever

There will be no

Fear or regret

Just one last

"I love you"

Sent from my soul

To yours

When it feels effortless
You've found the right one
When you apply effort anyway
They've found the right one

She knows

The darkness in me

That I won't even

Write about

But she still

Falls asleep

In my arms

She gets this look

In her eyes

When something

Excites her

That look

Is the something

That excites

Me

I have searched through
All of who I am
And all I can find
Is love for
All of who you are

I don't believe
There's any life
Beyond the ground
We're buried in
But I can face
That savage knife
If you'll decay
With me till then

The way she
Loves me
Makes me
Feel like
Mortality
Might be
A negative thing
After all

When she looks at herself
Her eyes are drawn
To her perceived imperfections
A little too much here
A stretch mark there
She will never understand
That when I look at her
The only thing I see
Is the most goddamn fun
I have ever had
In my entire fucking life

It's the way
You make me feel
Naked
When I am
Fully clothed
And make me feel
Safe
When I am completely
Naked

I do not miss

For a moment

Believing in magic

In the sky

That I could cry out to

When times are bad

But not having anyone

Or anything

That I can thank

For you

At times feels

Like an unbearable

Injustice

You will know

That you are perfect

For each other

When those

Inevitable moments

Of painful imperfection

Still don't make you question

How perfect you are

For each other

She is not my muse
I've never needed inspiration
But she's the only one
Who has never tried
To wrap my creativity in chains

She doesn't complete me
I've never needed to be added to
But she's never tried
To rip away
Even the smallest undesirable piece
Of who I am

She just loves me
Completely
Unconditionally
And somehow
She makes it look
Easy

I had never been loved before
But I thought I knew
What it would feel like
I had no idea
How good she would be
At loving me

It's nice to be forgiven
But it is far better
To be with someone
Who doesn't constantly
Make you feel like
You need to be forgiven
For simply being yourself

She makes me
Lock the doors
At night
And I
Sleep better knowing
She really believes
There might be
Something out there
Worse than
Me

We'll die together

Like the end of
The Notebook

But we'll be naked

HOW IT SHOULD FEEL

Everything inside exposed and laid bare
Your ribcage spread wide to allow them to stare
At every single piece of your own unique dysfunction
Every fear, every hope, all the shame and perversion
Every lie you wrap yourself in to somehow survive
All the terrible things in there you're too exhausted to
    hide
Give them every possible reason to be appalled and run
    away
Show them every single reason no one else could ever
    stay…

But they do, as if there's something wrong inside them,
    too
Like the messed up pieces of you could somehow help
    them make it through
And it feels like every random cell in history conspired
To make you both the kind of wreck the other one de-
    sired
All of time and space, it seems, have plotted this some-
    how
And you see every bit of pain collaborate to make right
    now
It should feel far more intense than words could ever

explain
All the poets try, but you know their efforts are in
vain

That's how it feels

She doesn't freak out
When my eyes wander
That's why
My body never will

My cynical lack of belief

Makes it hard to speak

Of *meant-to-be*s

But if by Providence

Anything ever was conceived

It would have to be

The bond between

You and me

It's the way it feels
Like you are inside of me
When I'm inside you

I wanted you so badly
For so long
But when I finally got that chance
I tried as hard as I could
To show you every possible reason
That you should just walk away
I let you crawl into every dark corner
You danced with every skeleton
In every closet inside me…

And you didn't walk away
You just loved me
And that's all I ever wanted

It's just a place
But all of it
Reminds me of you
So it's my favorite place

A picture is worth a thousand words
Unless you are in love
And you feel as if you might die
If you can't express that love
Then you're going to need some words
Every single word you know
And then you'll want to learn more words
And after that
You will seriously consider
Making up new words
To somehow explain the intensity of what you are
    feeling
And you will never really be able to do it
Even with all those words
But they'll get you a lot closer
Than a picture ever will

Isn't it ironic
How finally finding someone
Who loves you
Exactly as you are
Can make you want to be
A better person
Just for them?

Loving you

And being loved by you

Is by far

The easiest thing I have ever done

But I am still a man

Who has been built for

The battles of life

I thrive on the struggles

I feed on the difficult and sometimes frightening
    situations in life

So do not think for a single second

That there is anything

That life may throw at us

That will ever weaken my resolve

To love you forever

Everything that's fucked up in you

Is perfect

For everything that's fucked up in me

You will never understand my level of commit-
ment to you
Or the amount of determination in me
To love you forever
I am a pit bull
A wolverine
A Tasmanian devil
I am a Spartan
A gladiator
A Navy SEAL
I am the fucking Terminator
And I absolutely
Will
Not
Stop
Loving you
Ever
Until you are dead
And then I will rip a hole
Through time and space
And follow you
Wherever your beautiful soul is launched to
And love you for eternity

We've almost made love

In reality

As many times as we made love

In my imagination

Before we were together

My imagination

Drastically underestimated you

You love me
You really do
Every messed-up part of me
It's not something I feel
It's something I know
So I swear
For the rest of my life
I will wish on every star in the sky
I will throw every penny I earn
Into a wishing well
I will blow out the candles
On strangers' children's birthday cakes
And I will wish
A million times
Just one wish…

That whatever the fuck is wrong with you
Will never be cured

You are the best thing that ever happened

To anyone

And you happened

To me

It feels as if I've always loved you
From birth
Or maybe even before that
But that part of me
The very best part of me
Laid dormant
Asleep
Until I finally found you

You didn't just crawl inside
And look at all my dark corners
And love everything you saw there
That would have been enough
That would have been more
Than anyone else has ever done for me
But you didn't stop there
You allowed me
And encouraged me
To start dragging all my demons
Out into the light
And in that light
They really don't look like demons at all
They look like children
And I love them
And I love you for making that happen

And then it happened
You happened
And it all made sense
And I finally understood
What that terrible feeling
Deep within me
My entire life was:
It was the absence of you

We were broken

By life

By others

By our own serious dysfunctions

But we finally found each other

After almost two decades

Of near misses

Of being so close

And when we finally did come together

All of the jagged edges

Of our broken pieces

Fit together perfectly

As if all that time

We were being broken

So we would be perfect

For each other

I've built myself for pain

An emotional badass

Forged by the pressures of life

And the fires of hell

Scarred flesh stretched across

A cast-iron chest cavity

Completely

Fucking

Invincible

But I never thought to prepare myself for this

Love

And the way it simultaneously breathes life into
    your soul

And sucks the air right out of your lungs

The intense pleasure of a true lover's presence

Followed by the excruciating pain of their absence

I really thought I was prepared for anything

But the deluge of tears

Just barely held back

Tell me I was very wrong

I'm not sure what you did

But apparently

It made me

Forget to

Breathe

I TOLD YOU SO

You know what they're all going to think
Don't you?
We are a dream team
Of high hopes
Dysfunction
And failure
Even now
The *I-told-you-so*s
Are beating the backs of their teeth to death
Begging for the moment
They can gleefully be hurled at us
But you and I both know
They will certainly die
With those words
Still dancing behind their lips

She is heaven

Laced with

Brimstone

This will happen sometimes
On our way to forever
Together
In the middle of our fairy tale
Some very un-fairy tale shit will happen
And it will be hard
And for a moment
It might not feel like love at all
But I will always apologize
And I will always forgive
And I will always hold your face and kiss you
And we will always move on together
Right back into our regularly scheduled
Fairy tale

Inner beauty and outer beauty

Are often spoken of

As if they are

Mutually exclusive

But there are those rare creatures

Who possess a mind-blowing inner beauty

Wrapped in an incredible outer beauty

That can keep a person thinking

Ridiculously inappropriate thoughts

Every moment

Of every single day

I know these creatures exist

Because I have found one

And there is not a human alive

Who can rightfully consider themselves

Luckier than I

Saying, "Good morning"

Without saying

Anything at all

That is how

Great days begin

It's a terrible feeling
When you spend every second
Of every fucking day
Trying to hide
How much you hate yourself
From yourself
And everyone else
And then your walls fall down
For just a moment
And someone you love
Has to see what you really are
But when that person
Doesn't run away
And doesn't hate you
For hating yourself
It can also feel
Pretty goddamn wonderful

Tell her she's beautiful
And that you love her
Then pull her hair
And smack her ass
It's not rocket science

The smallest actions
Often scream
"I love you"
The loudest

The saddest thing

Is realizing

That she's been

Treated so badly

It's going to

Take a while

Before she learns

Not to be surprised

When I treat her right

All those years

She was right down the road

Walking distance

Feeling just as alone

And unloved

As I did

That will always sting

What could we both have been

If we had been loved like this

All along?

It's all good now

And we are happy

But those what-ifs

Can be a motherfucker

They would have had you
Caged and chained
Insecure boys
Hiding in grown men's bodies
Who could not handle
All of who you are
Who felt the need
To control what you wore
And where you went
With whom...
You are free now
Because I am secure
In who I am
And who you are
And what this love is
And I know exactly what you will do
With every bit of freedom I can give you
You will run straight into my arms
And stay there
Forever

It feels like
Making love
But looks like
Making war

OPEN BOOK

I'm an open book
In a culture
That doesn't
Fucking
Read

HOW TO TAKE A SELFIE, IN FOUR HAIKU

I am Alpha Male
And god of fuck to mask my
Insecurities

I'm a soul that's frail
And skin that's rough, stretched across
My impurities

I'm a dead-end stare
That hides the tears I've held for
Seems like centuries

I am cock and flair
To mask my fears, and words to
Cleanse my memories

You think the use of

Profanity

Is the sign of an

Unintelligent mind?

Well

I have considered

All the words

In my extensive

Vocabulary

And I have decided to respond thusly:

Fuck

You

If it's important

To me

Don't tell me

It's not

Important

If indeed it is true

That great minds think alike

Then it would also

Logically hold true that

Not-so-great minds think alike as well

So get over yourself

The fact that everyone in your

Echo chamber

Agrees with each other

Does not mean that

Any of you

Have a great mind

I will certainly fail you
If your expectations for me
Are anything other than
What I already know
That I am

Your problem
Not mine

If you don't

Absolutely adore them

And worship

The ground they walk on

Even in their

Weakest

Darkest times

Then you don't really

Love them at all

And you certainly

Don't deserve

To get to be in their presence

During their

Strongest

Brightest moments

Plastic roses bloom
In my soul chamber's crawlspace
Broken moments fade

I'm sure someone did it to you

A young girl in rural Kentucky

Your daddy

Or a sneaky uncle

Or a neighbor

And they left you with a lifelong tension

Between lust

And love

And you gave it to me

I never knew your name

And as much as I remember about that night

After 33 years

I can't see your face

But I think of you often

When I'm thinking of things

That made me

And I sincerely hope

That you are doing well

My greatest moments
Have always happened
Right after I was broken
Because I put all the pieces
Back where I wanted them

PLAYGROUND

I cannot breathe
I cannot see
What you did to me
I can't believe

All that's left of me
Is what you left of me
Ever since that night and every other night
Tonight, tonight, tonight
All that once was mine
Has now been left behind
Ever since that game and every other game
We play, we play, we play

We play, we play, but it's not a game
You played with me and caused all this pain

I can't believe I let you ruin me
You used my naiveté to strip me of my dignity
I can't believe I let you bury me
You used my humility to strip me of my identity

I've fed pieces
Of my heart
And my soul
To those who spit it back in my face
Because I'm not their favorite flavor

BIRTHRIGHT

My daddy never taught me a thing
Except the art of running away
I just wish he would have taken the shame
Of his inferior DNA
The apple never falls far
From the tree that gave it a name
And a name change can't do a thing
When you're exactly the same
The wounds heal but the scar
Is like a slap in the face
The pain's gone, but in its wake
A hollow I can't replace
My birthright is the demons
I face everyday
Finding solace in the hope that somewhere
He feels exactly the same

You don't get to live the life I've lived
Do the things I've done
Survive
The things I've survived
Without having to wear that past
All over you
For the rest of your life
That's just not how it works

Sway

So hypnotic

Back and forth

Fingers in eyes

Until the rage dies down

Until the pain subsides

Tears on sleeve

Back and forth

So hypnotic

Sway

Can we give up
On humanity
Without losing our own?

In the darkest corners

Of my nihilistic mind

I know that survival

For its own sake

Is the only reason

We are here

But having someone

To do that

Almost-certainly-pointless

Surviving

With

Makes it a lot easier

To pretend that

Life has

Meaning

I've swallowed
A sea of pride
But I still can't
Wash the taste
Of failure and regret
From my tongue

I've laid on more rock-bottoms than most
Incarceration
Homelessness
Addiction
But what I saw in her face that night
And the fact that she would never say it aloud
The realization that I wasn't being the man
That the woman I need more than anything need-
    ed...
That was the hardest, lowest rock-bottom
I've ever landed on

I've built my walls up
Thick and high
Out of every piece
Of my will to survive
But if something, somehow
Gets inside
It can't get out
Until it dies

We've auctioned ourselves off

One piece of who we are at a time

For a kiss

For a touch

For a love

For a fuck

For a pat on the back

And the tip of a hat

And when there's just nothing left

And we're scattered and vexed

We can't find the whole

Without the pieces we've sold

I've never once blamed you
Whatever the fuck your name was
Even when every therapist
And 12-step leader
I ever had
Told me I had every right
You were twice my age
But what would that have been?
Ten?
Twelve maybe?
Just a child
Just like me
Even then I knew
Someone else did this to both of us
But on this fucking day
As I lose the battle against the fallout
Of what you did
I'm finally ready to say
Fuck you
For ruining me
Forever

All of the best things

About me

Only exist

Because of the worst things

About me

I think I just prayed
Or maybe it was a wish
I don't believe in either one
So it was probably
Just the whimper
Of an exhausted soul
That desperately needs
Something
Anything
To go right

We all feel the same pain
On the way to the same grave
But rather than an embrace
We all hate in the same way

I was the light
Buried in your skin
I was the innocence
Before your heart was filled with sin
I was the cage
So cold where you have dwelt
I was the rage
The only source of warmth you felt

You made me that night
With the glow of a kerosene heater
Bouncing off the walls
I was far too young to understand
That I was being used
Too mesmerized by
The wiggling nakedness of a female body
And the taste
Of someone else's saliva
On my tongue
I will probably never
Fully understand
How much you fucked me
When you fucked me
But from that moment on
I became a sineater
Of godlike proportions
Swallow it down and lock it inside
Absorb every blow
From everyone
A whipping boy who
Will
Not
Break
Yeah…
You fucked me pretty good

THAT'S NOT POETRY

But you also taught me what my purpose is and
   always will be
And I'm pretty goddamn good at it

I win more than I lose
But I could use a reprieve
From the everyday wars
I must wage against me

Sifting through my own decay
Nightmares replayed while I'm awake
Repaint myself in darker shades
To match the world around me

These heartstrings often feel like chains
Contradicting everything my weary brain
Knows will keep me safe from pain
As I face the world around me

I don't bleed ink
I know because
I've seen what I bleed
Pouring from my wrist
In crimson waves
It was definitely just
Blood

At the age of 9
You could find me
Hiding
In a dark library
Reading human sexuality textbooks
By 11
I had figured out how to
Hide a woman's magazine
Inside a *Sports Illustrated*
At the supermarket
And read the sexually frustrated
Letters to the editor
I was just a boy
But I was learning everything
That men were doing wrong
With a naked woman
I was determined
To be a sex machine
A **GOD** of **FUCK**
I was learning how to give a woman
A near-deadly amount
Of orgasms
Maybe then
Someone
Would love me

I have cauterized

Far too many wounds

In this fragile heart

It still beats

It still feels

For the most part

But you'll have to forgive me

If it's not as sensitive

As it once was

It's not difficult to be
"Down to earth"
When you've never
Spent enough time
Off the ground
To knock the dirt off

Our nation has become

A parody of itself

A caricature

More grotesque

Than humorous

A joke

That's just too real

To laugh at

After years in a
Self-induced fog
This sunshine is blinding
Almost frightening
My chest relaxing and tightening
Senses heightening
But still in a place
Far short of enlightening
I'm still waiting for these
Moments of clarity
To feel a little less
Disorienting

No one ever knows it
When I fall apart in here
I've built my ramparts thick and high
Then strengthened them for years
So when the darkness takes me
And renders meaning moot
My defenses persist of their own volition
Like a haunted armor suit

I've never had control

Marionette chains throw me about

In a dance that I don't know

I'm a soul

Riding a meat roller coaster

Let go

Ant throw

Weary hands to the sky

My many masters know my pain

And laugh in disdain

Laid to blade

Laid to flame

Laid to rest

All that's left

A stone engraved

With a puppet's name

If I become

Too much to hold

Please just

Put me down

It's not your job

To make me whole

And I promise

I won't drown

"Let me buy you a drink"
I'd say to me
With a grin and a wink
But we both knew
It would take more than one
To make me think
I looked like someone
I'd want to take home
With me

This is where
It finds you
Every time
3 a.m.
Lights out
Staring at the night

HOW TO MAKE A MONSTER

The smell of coal reminds me of the monsters that we made
Scribbled works of art, I guess some memories never fade
Kerosene reminds me of the monster I became
This whole world had changed, replacing innocence with
SHAME

The devil smokes a cigarette and watches from the wall
His velvet grin turns into mocking laughter at my fall
The air around me thickens as a giant hand descends
I bury all this deep inside, my brokenness begins

My eyes were pried wide open
Before I was prepared to see
Infecting a little child
With full-grown insecurity

This
Is how
You make
A monster

Look at what you made

117

There is a very fine line

Between a legitimate reason

And a pathetic excuse

If I'm honest with myself

I think I'm standing

Right on that line

I really have been

Fucked up pretty bad

But I'm also probably

Just a piece of shit

A GLIMMER OF HOPE

I wither
Fissures slither like rivers
Growing bigger
In my once-strong armor
That now twists and quivers
Bitter voices whisper
As winter shivers
Beg to differ
With even the faintest
Of hope's glimmers

I did not gaze upon
That delicious forbidden fruit
And then defiantly
Pluck it and partake
I was force-fed
At the age of 5
While a voyeuristic deity
Watched and licked his lips
I'll not be judged
For his apathy

CRUMBLE

I was a volatile virtuoso
Of living vicariously through you
You were the star, so I was the also
Nonexistent. Invisible. See-through.

It took me a while to perceive how vile
My worship of you was just hatred disguised
But I was the one who, so full of bile
Projected on you the me I despised

Somber, creased brow like solemn stigmata
Self-hatred infects and hastens demise
No peace inside, no hope for nirvana
The darkness breaks through this shell I despise

This fist-fucked façade falls off and reveals
The cancerous core I've tried to conceal

ATONEMENT

ATONEMENT

Once again I feel the flame that I fight to contain
Every word that I know falls short of my will to explain
The pain grows till it's larger than the walls of my chest
My throat swells, holding back the sins I haven't confessed
It's like a razor blade that slices everything that I am
Everything that I hate, because I know that I'm damned
A blackened heart turns once-red blood to a darker shade
I've tasted grace but then decided I don't want to be saved

My life replayed through dreams I have in waking moments
Left alone when I was broken
Now walk away without atonement

RECANT

I've felt that subtle rise of hate
Bow down and obey the deity
But it could never get past my face
Because I never forgot what freedom means

Discard the chains that I put on willfully
My only sin was ever believing in sin
Untie the knots that I tied so skillfully
I can't believe I let you under my skin

My eyes are bloodshot red
And every hair stands on end
Denied myself just like you said
All by myself when I needed a friend

But I can still hear your voice in my skull
Like the ghost of someone who never lived
And when I think I need help with my soul
I remember every time that you never did

Caskets and cradles and demons and angels
Are blurred till they all seem the same
The righteous, the saints, will all line up to take
Whatever they can from your veins
Then when they are through, none of you left to use
They retreat to the shelter of grace
But you're left in the wake, with the pain and the rage
And no strength to resuscitate faith

You're not a damn saint
Holy skin stretched across vile
Meat that rots like mine

There was a very specific moment
Snorting a pain pill
Off the toilet in the men's room
Between teaching Sunday school class
And attending the main service
That I realized
Perhaps I was a junkie
I'm better now
I don't snort pills anymore
Or go to church

I did not leave
The flock of believers
Just to join
Another flock
Of unbelievers

I'm almost certain that "enlightenment"
Is just as ridiculous
A concept
As a belief in an eternity in heaven
But when you can perform
The mind-numbingly mundane
Everyday tasks of life
With a smile on your face
And a happy song in your heart
Then you're probably as close
To either one of those things
As the human condition will allow
You are also probably
In love

Beware the godly
They hurt whoever they want
And run back to grace

It is one of life's little ironies

That you can lose every belief

That you once held dear

And somehow

For the first time

Come to understand

What faith really feels like

Wrath of God?
You say that so much
It doesn't mean
Anything
Anymore

A voyeuristic sadist
Watches all of this
With phallus gripped
And malice lips
A grin
Crescendos to
A thunderous laugh

"I can't believe
They still believe
I'll save them"

NAKED

See my face

So empty

But there are demons inside me

So now I

Release them

My twisted sick purity

Undress this

Infected

Heart full of hate on display

Sadistic

Afflicted

Intrinsic value of me

There's no cure but death for me so my disease is now uncaged

I'm impure and festering, so come and see my naked rage

Insecure and all alone, nobody answers when I pray

Lost my nerve and will to live, now all that's left: tears on a page

"God gave you these beautiful children"

Um

Ok

How do I put this delicately?

You see

When two people really love each other

Or maybe when they are inebriated

They…

Never mind

You wouldn't believe me if I told you

Yes

Babies fall from the fucking sky

Did you just say
"Homosexuals are an abomination"?
Oh, I bet you are
A fucking maniac
In bed...

ADAM

I always loved you, cousin
Even during that really dark time
When I loved Jesus
Way too much
To associate with a queer like you
I loved you
And when that whole life
Turned out to be
Someone else's huge lie
And Jesus was nowhere to be found
You were there
Without hesitation
And you loved me
In one of my darkest hours
I have no doubt
I wouldn't have made it without you
So I'm sorry
For ever thinking that maybe I was better than you
Because I'm not
But you do make me want to be better than I am
Thank you

Despite what you think
Don't call this a fall from grace
Bitch, I'm skydiving

I probably could have
Held onto my faith
If I had been able
To look back and see those
Footprints in the sand
Where a loving deity
Had walked beside me
And even carried me
When I was too weak
But when I looked back
There were no footprints at all
There was only a ditch in that sand
Marking the path
Where I had dragged myself
All by myself
All along

I feel the fire of Gehenna

Residing in me

And wormwood bitters

All the blood that I bleed

So run me through

With righteous blade

I'll accept no grace

For being

How I was made

Just call it a

Quirk

Or call it a

Personality flaw

Call it

The ill-fated offspring

Of a fling

Between

Nature and nurture

But don't call it a

Demon

Because you and I both know

Those motherfuckers don't breathe

So you've just anointed

That thing you claim

You want to defeat

With immortality

That fire you hold
That is hate for my soul
Will never consume
The guilt in your own

The impious eyes of my own reflection
Stare back at me
I believe nothing is sacred
Yet I still feel unholy
Blasphemous and profane
The ghosts of dogmas long dead
Dance through dark places in my skull
They tell me I'm wrong and impure
And it excites me
And when my intellect tries to
Rationalize my "sins" by reminding me
That I don't even believe in sin
I won't let it
It's just so much more exciting
To pretend that maybe there is
Some ancient cosmic morality
That I am boldly thumbing my nose at

With righteous teeth
We rip our pound of flesh
From those who've caused us pain
Then beg for mercy
We've not shown
When they line up to do the same

I am not a man of faith
But I am not entirely faithless
I do not believe in gods or heavens
But I do make myself believe
That good things can happen
And silly things like love really matter
As irrational as those beliefs seem at times
Because without that bare minimum
Amount of faith
It starts to feel like I'm just
Running out the clock
On a very pointless existence
And I can't face the day
On those terms

I'm going to get
A great deal of pleasure
Out of sharing hell
With all these goddamn saints

In that moment
With tears pouring
Down my face
And my soul heavy
With the knowledge
That I simply did not possess
The emotional strength
To do what I sincerely felt
Was the right thing to do
Praying more fervently
Than I had ever prayed before
I finally realized
There wasn't going to be
Any magic to help me get through
And logically
I knew that could only mean
One of two things
Either my mystical best friend
Was nothing more than
A figment of my imagination
Or just wasn't that into me
Either way
I felt like a fool
And I ended it right there
Forever

The most
"Christ-like"
Thing anyone
Has ever done
For me
Was done by
A Muslim

We preach to our choirs
And bask in *Amen*s
While thriving on every
"Fuck you" of dissent
With voices and fists raised
In self-righteous rage
We'll all face our grave
Without a single mind changed

Every single prayer

Was answered with a "lesson"

So I stopped praying

I'm surrounded by a million motherfuckers who fall short of the standard in me

The voices in my head won't let me sleep through the ignorance I see

The world turns and gets worse in spite of every angry word that I say

Nothing changed when I prayed so I replaced it with rage

You can't taste peace without the tongue of a fool

If He's really up there
And He really cares
Then you're going to be O.K.
Right?
But you know what else is true?
Even if He's not up there
Or He doesn't care
You're still going to be
Just fucking fine

Give no fucks
And take no shit
This is the path
To inner peace

DELICIOUS VOID

The earth's crust opens up to reclaim what it owns
Everything that I've been disappears as they cover
my bones
There's no tunnel
No light
No judgment
No Christ
No fire
No plight
No wrong
And no right
Beyond the frustration of day
And the terror of night
A delicious void closes tight
And the last pieces of me form an exhausted smile
As my life disappears with one last, relieved sigh

Death is not a sentence
Life is

All this animated worm food
But we do think
We are quite special
Don't we?

HUMAN

You know what's going to happen

And you know it's going to hurt like hell

And when it's over

Another piece of you will be gone

And you'll cry into a pillow

And move on

But you do it anyway

Because someone else needs you to

And you put their needs

Before your own instincts

Because you are human

And you're pretty fucking good at it

I hate those who hate
I absolutely do not tolerate
Intolerance
I judge the judgmental
And I
Dogmatically oppose dogma
I'm pretty much better
Than all you motherfuckers

If every star in the sky

Belonged to me

And every grain of sand in the sea

Were mine

And I traded them all

For middle fingers

I still would not possess enough

*Fuck you*s

To express how much I loathe you

Words don't escape me
But there are those rare moments
When I escape them

Sometimes I breathe
In a way that feels like
A first breath
In a way that feels like
Being alive
Then I forget
How I did it

DANCING IN THE RAIN

So many times I've felt completely damaged be-
   yond repair
As if the brief moments when I thought I cared
Were nothing more than phantom pain from a
   limb that wasn't there

Just a costume I wear
That could never hide the despair
Revealed in a dead-end stare

But there are those moments that let me know this
   heart is indeed alive
When it feels more than just what's necessary to
   simply breathe and survive
Those moments I know, beneath a chest that's
   calcified
There's still a heart that longs for love, it's thus far
   been denied

Sometimes these moments cause as much pain as
   joy inside
And make me wonder if it was wise to share the
   things that I confide
But I'll never regret a single time I've opened up

and tried
Because I'd rather stand in a storm than be afraid
to go outside.

We like to talk
About our "demons"
Such poetic imagery
But when I look at
What I hate inside
Every bit of it
Is just me

It's not that I don't value
Legitimate advice about love
But there's something about
Your passionless dead-end stare
That leads me to believe
Perhaps
You may not be
An authority on the subject

You should know
That my opinion of you
Is based entirely on your
Opinion of me
So by all means
Tell me what you think
Is wrong with me

It has been my experience

That honesty

And humility

Are very often

Mutually exclusive

So really

Which would you prefer?

There will be no peace
The human animal
Is far better
At doing animal shit
Than all the other animals

The more I experience
The things that humans
Are capable of
The more I am enamored
With the concept of
Karma

The line between
Being honest
And being an asshole
Is a very fine line indeed
You are just a fucking asshole
Stop trying to pretend
It is a virtue

Please don't assume
That you must have been through
More than I have
Just because I make
Manufacturing a will to live
Look sexy as fuck

Measuring phallus with flannel and ink
The truth is revealed by insecure gaze
Pretense and whiskey grant false sense of strength
That reeks of malaise when etched in a page

Caricature begets caricature
Inbreed Bukowski till all meaning dies
Poetry's not dead, it's simply immured
Hipster-shaped boxes don't come in my size

Your definition of "real poetry"
Excludes all who don't remind you of you
You can't comprehend the realness I bleed
Because the real you stays wrapped in untruth

Point your satirical hatred at me
Let's see which one of us leaves with our teeth

Many years ago
I had an enlightenment experience
Where I understood how connected
We all are
When the acid wore off
I realized I don't really want
To be connected to
Most of you
Motherfuckers

I am not predisposed
To arrogance or conceit
I've overcome a crippling self-hatred
And nonexistent self-esteem
That almost killed me in my youth
Even now
There are far too many
Wretched and disgusting things about me
That I am all too painfully aware of
But when I look around at our culture
And grade myself against that curve
I'm a solid fucking A-plus
Every goddamn day of the week

We entertain ourselves

With the stories of monsters

Because we desperately want to believe

There might be something

More terrifying

Than humanity

She shouldn't have to be

Your mom

Or your sister

Or your wife

Or your daughter

She is a **WOMAN**

And if you were

A fucking man

You would know that

The monsters
Under my bed
Are terrified
Of what's above them

Ladies

Stop comparing yourself

To other women

God made you all

Different

And beautiful

And wonderful

In your own special ways

Now

Make out with each other

You've absorbed
A thousand blows
From the stones
They've thrown
But they'll still swear
You're the monster
If you return
What they've sown

If you do not possess

The intelligence or maturity

To be able to ascertain

If a woman wants to

Have sex with you

Then keep your fucking dick

In your pants

Until you are a

Grown-ass man

Mother nature

Is an invincible

War machine

You want

The whole world

And one day

In grotesque

Decomposing repose

You will be

One with it

I'm not frightened
By the darkness of night
But by the things
My mind does
Without the distraction
Of sight

My head and my heart
Are almost never at odds
I either have
A real fucking smart heart
Or an emotional fucking head
The problem has never been
My head
Or my heart
The problem is
There is something else in me
That is neither head nor heart
That is not even me at all
And my head and heart
Can't seem to defeat it

All the monsters
Tell their therapists
About the times
They were victims

We dream of making
The world a better place,
But most of its problems
Hide behind our own face.

I have lived in a Southern hell
My entire life
And I fucking hate it
I do know many people
Whose horizons have stretched
Substantially further than my own
They have all told me
That people suck
No matter where you go
You only find different kinds of assholes
They're probably right
But I would toss a fat man's salad right now
For the opportunity to find out
What life is like somewhere else
Anywhere else

The other monsters smile
Far more than I do
They don't know they're monsters
But I've always known the truth

We dismiss

Their concern

With a well-rehearsed

"I'm fine"

While searching

For strength

To inhale

One more time

I'm not certain it is a good thing
That our demons
Play so nicely together
I fear we may
Never feel the need
To defeat them

They feverishly
Scribbled down
The pain
As if
Their demons
Could be
Exorcised
To page
And sent away

"Aren't you worried about
What happens when you die?"
People dig holes every day
Someone will figure it out

I have something to tell you
And you're not going to like it
This world will never change
People are never going to get better
There will always be suffering
There will always be hatred
You cannot do anything to change that
But you?
You can change you
And that's an awful lot of power to have
In this world that otherwise leaves us
Feeling almost completely powerless

It seems all the lambs
Are wolves in disguise
And many wolves' eyes
Hide a lamb inside

We stare into
The darkness
And fight
The realization
That we are constructed
Of the exact same material

We all have life debris

Baggage

Things we've done

Or that have been done to us

That we carry around

And allow to shape the way we view the present

And the way we act in the present

We've got to put that shit down

"Let it go," they say

And it's true

But some of that debris is persistent

It doesn't just feel like baggage

It feels like part of who we are

So we may let it go today

And wake up tomorrow to find it staring us in the
face again

Let it go

Again

Today, tomorrow, and the next day

Every day until you're dead if need be

But don't ever let it control you

You are not your past

You are your present

I'm sorry
But you should know
The universe
Only revolves around you
In direct proportion
To your proximity
To me

Everyone says
They want
Honesty
But most of them
Are lying
When they say it

Bittersweet memories

Run through our heads

We're the travelers, the frozen

The ones left for dead

A monolithic randomness

Has tossed us all about

And we're so tired from the past in us

We just cannot get out

Red brushstrokes color everything

The curses of our fate

Wasting time still running

From the things we should embrace

All our youth and aspirations

Have disappeared beyond the sun

All that's left:

Determined breaths

To somehow

Live

Before we're done

Don't let the fact
That there are
Demons in this world
Make you lose sight
Of all the beautiful angels

Empathic whores

Carry a dreadful burden

For far too long

No, pumpkin
You do not have
"Demons inside"
If that were the case
All we would have to do
Is get a priest to roll off an altar boy
Just long enough to perform an exorcism
Sadly
You are your own fucking problem
But you are also
The solution

Do not speak of freedom
In reverent tones
If the only freedom you value
Is your own

The only thing worse

Than a bad man

Is a

Bad man

Who has figured out

How to convince those around him

That he is a good guy

My tongue bleeds
From teeth
That hold words beneath
But you still believe
I speak
Too freely

SOMEWHERE BETWEEN...

Somewhere between
The ball gag
And the strap-on
I realized…
Not all fairy tales
Look alike

I suppose it was my fault, really
When I said I was into
Smacking and choking
I should have clarified
That I didn't mean I wanted that shit done to me
So when you grabbed my throat
And smacked my face
Well
It frightened me a little bit

P.S. Ok. I'm still willing to try it
A dozen or so more times
Before I decide I'm definitely not into it.

xoxo

I love it when
We hold each other
So tight that
It feels like we are
Trying to occupy
The same space
The laws of physics
Will always prevent that
Of course
But it's really fun
To try

Shed no tears

For the Phoenix that crashes

Some of us were built

To play in these ashes

I was home-schooled

For religious reasons

I think the goal

Was to make sure

I never found out about

Drugs

Alcohol

Tattoos

Female orgasms

Or BBC porn...

It was worth a shot I guess

With our craniums

Ribcages

And legs

Spread wide

We write

And that vulnerability

Is our greatest strength

All of my favorite poets

Have their own

Very distinctive

And beautiful

Style

Fuck you guys

You are a woman
And I am a man
But I think
Perhaps
With a little effort
And creativity
We could still be
An abomination

She is
Simultaneous
Poetry and perversion
Like a sonnet
Wearing a strap-on

I hope we never fight

I mean

Really

We should

Never

EVER

Fight

Because if we ever have make-up sex

One of us is going to get fucking killed

And I'm too goddamn pretty

To go to prison

You say it's sexy
To watch me when I'm down there
But I'm sure it really just looks
Like I am trying
To lick the windows
Out of a bus

I thought of a really sensual poem

So I searched the internet for

"Black and white erotica"

To use as a backdrop

Sweet Mary, mother of fuck

Now I need a cigarette

And I forget my goddamn poem

Your children are not

A masterpiece

That you create

They are their own masterpieces

Creating themselves

And you have been given

The privilege

Of watching them

Be the artist

HOW TO BE A POET
IN FOUR HAIKU

A copious dose
Of whiskey-soaked self loathing
I'm a poet now

So vexed and morose
Chain smoking while composing
I'm a poet now

Fuck like Bukowski
Old typewriters arouse me
I'm a poet now

Just one thing missing
Why don't my readers "get me"?
I'm a poet now

Through years of

Deeply honest self-examination

I have determined that I am at least

89% straight

I mean

I could just swim around in

Bradley Cooper's eyes

For days…

But I probably don't want to touch his dick

Perhaps
I could understand
What you're trying to say
If you weren't
Gagging on
Bukowski's cock

Oh, thank fuck!
I thought you might not
Be into that anymore
After the wedding

As a very young boy
My first crush was
Boy George
For some reason
The words
"Boy" and "George"
Did not communicate to me
That perhaps
He was not a woman

Remember that time
When one of us
(You, not me)
Forgot the protocol
And for fifteen seconds
That felt like an eternity
I watched your seemingly dying
Twitching body
Lying on the bed
With your eyes rolled back
And my first thought was
"I'm going to prison"
And my second thought was
"I bet they're into this shit in prison"
Can we do that again sometime?

Make love to her
With your poems
And your words
With your mind and your soul
With almost everything you have
But with your cock…
Just fuck her
To the gates of hell and back
Pull her hair and smack her ass
Leave her quivering and breathless
Wondering what the fuck kind of beast
Just plowed through her
And for fuck's sake, pumpkin
Don't write a goddamn poem about it
If you can't deliver

Put my phone down and be sociable?

Fuck you

I'm only pretending to write a poem right now

So no one will think

I'm available for a conversation

Ladies
Being submissive in the bedroom
Is pretty fucking awesome
(I mean, if you're into that sort of thing)
But everywhere else
Give
Him
Hell
Stand toe-to-toe with him
And make it very clear that a few ounces
Of male genitalia
Do not translate into any form of rank
In YOUR fucking world
If he does not thrive on the opportunity
To walk through life with an equal by his side
Then leave that motherfucker where he stands
And go find a real man who does
Trust me
If he is so insecure that he needs to feel like the boss
With his clothes on
There is no fucking way
He will be a boss with his clothes off

I like to think of myself

As a sapiosexual,

But big asses

Are pretty damn appealing too

I suppose there may be
Some problems
That just can't be fixed
With ridiculously
Filthy
Sex
But I think
We owe it to ourselves
To at least try that first
Just in case

She's the kind of girl
You don't have to clean
Your browser history for

Ladies
If he is not capable
Of making his own
Goddamn sandwich
Then there is no fucking way
He is going to find
The G-spot

Your hips move
Like they know
Your ass
Is fabulous

I wrote the perfect poem
But I can't let you read it
If you read it
You might like it
And if you like it
Some other motherfucker
Might like it
And if too many
Motherfuckers like it
Then these other motherfuckers
Won't like it
And if those motherfuckers
Don't like it
Then it must not be
The perfect poem...
So I wrote the perfect poem
But I can't let any
Of you motherfuckers
Read it

He's the kind of guy
Who calls all the other artists
"Artists"
Just so you will know
That he
Is a real fucking artist

If you spend most of your time
Writing about
What other writers
Are writing about
You are not a writer
You are a fucking critic

I think far too highly
Of myself
To spend my life
With someone
Who no one else
Would want
So jealousy
Is not an option

I think most people feel it

In a gaze

Or a touch

A kind gesture

Or an embrace

But I've only felt it

In lusting

Thrusting

Fucking

Breathless and twitching

Sweating and flinching

Smacking and pinching

Tongue covered in someone else's

Everything…

I might not understand

What love really means

I should probably hide
The fifty feet of rope
And the riding crop
That's lying in the corner
So none of the children
Think they are getting
A fucking pony for Christmas

Go fuck myself?
You say that as if
It would be
An unpleasant
Proposition

Sometimes

When two broken people

Are trying to

Put each other

Back together

It might look an awful lot

Like they are trying to

Completely destroy each other…

If they are doing it right

My wife mentioned
Role-playing last night
And my first thought was
Dungeons and Dragons
Apparently
I'm an even bigger nerd
Than I am
A pervert

She's the kind of girl
Who makes me forget
To give a fuck
That all the real poets
Are going to hate my
She-poem

From the very first moment
He becomes aware
Of his dangling phallic digit
Everything a boy will do
Is an attempt to prove
He has the biggest

No, pumpkin
She is not
"Chaos"
She's just
Far too complicated
For your simple ass
To understand

UNDEFEATED

UNDEFEATED

You've been abandoned and back-handed
Molested
Rejected
Infested
And still left with
A heart of gold that gets stronger when tested

A thousand betrayals couldn't make you want to do the same
You've tried and you've failed, well acquainted with shame
You refuse to be changed and welcome the inevitable pain
You've tasted what you thought was love, and learned it was only
   a game

You've cried in the rain until tears turned to laughter
Then walked away after like none of it mattered
You're so used to the cold that your teeth never chatter
And you relish the challenge when your whole world is shattered

You are undefeated
Not because you never lose
But because every time you do
You choose to become
A better version of you

Remember

Flowers need

Both sunshine

And rain

To flourish

A little bit of

Bullshit

Doesn't hurt either

I am not proud of my skin

But I am proud of every single scar that decorates it

I am not proud that I was born with a cock

But I am proud of the way it can knock a fucking
cervix off its axis

I am not proud that I am attracted to women

But I am proud that I do not treat women like they
only exist to get me off

I have no pride in any group or sub-group

You could ever try to squeeze me into

I am a goddamn individual

And I am pretty fucking proud of myself

It will never matter
How many people
Believe you are capable
Of great things
If one of those people
Isn't you

I like to chase that thing I feel inside
I try to pinpoint exactly where it hides

That nagging little spot that's always needing
    more
Needs a drug, needs a lover, needs a hug, needs
    awards
Needs everything it doesn't have and can't be
    satisfied
With anything the here and now abundantly sup-
    plies
I close my eyes and try to find the source of all this
    pain
Searching every single place in me, I always find
    the same…

There's nothing there
The pain's not real
And everything's O.K.

You've convinced yourself
You're trapped
But the only thing
Holding you in place
Is your own
Stubborn grip

Just me

Poured out

Nothing more

Nothing less

No apologies

You keep looking for that missing piece
Of your missing peace
At the bottom line
At the bottom of a bottle
At the bottom of some ass
(Yes, they have a bottom, but you won't find what
    you're looking for there)
At the bottom of a cock
(You can do it; just relax)
At the bottom of every barrel
But what you are looking for
Is at the bottom of your own—
I'll call it a soul
And if you can't figure out how to get there
Then the only peace you will ever find
Will be at the bottom of a grave

In our own

Very special way

We are all

Just another

Cliché

The permanent foundation of who we are is poured with no input from us by the often-incompetent architects Nature and Nurture. By the time we are able to have some say in the construction of ourselves, the structure we have to work with is frequently unstable and offers very little protection from the elements of life. But with a little patience and a lot of hard work, we can perform enough small renovations to make our own bones finally feel like home.

I don't fight this hard
Because I think
The world can be changed
I fight this hard
To make damn sure
It doesn't
Change me

Life is mercilessly short
Even when it is not extinguished
Far too early by the tragedies
That are all too often
A part of the human condition
Regardless of what you believe
Happens when that last breath is exhaled
You only have a finite number of moments
In this body
On this planet
Please stop wasting them

There is a fine line

Between stoic acceptance

And just giving up

I'm not impressed by

Trophies and accomplishments

Dollars or degrees

Successful people

Are not interesting to me

Show me your failures

Show me your filth

Tell me how life has

Damn-near destroyed you

And left you bloody and broken

And gasping for breath

Tell of the wars you wage

On a daily basis

With yourself

Just to keep going

One more day

Tell me

You've barely fucking made it

This far

And you're really not sure

If you'll make it past this point…

Those are the stories

I like to hear

Do not allow

Your circumstances

To create

Who you are

Create yourself

Through your reactions

To your circumstances

In the darkness
And harshness
Of our lives
So imperfect
There are still
Love stories
And that
Makes it
Worth it

All these pieces of me
Mostly jagged and sharp
Crammed into a space
That is jaded and dark
But I've also found something
Resembling a heart
That is worth so much more
Than the sum of my parts

Don't you dare beg
Ever
Not for recognition
Or attention
Not love
Or affection
Not for safety
Or protection
Never beg for dick
Or an ass
Just do what you do
And make them all
Beg for you

When you come
To the realization
That you are
Unbreakable
Then you are
Free to love
With abandon

This world will leave
Its mark on you
Scarred flesh
And shattered soul
Stand tall
Wipe the blood off your lip
With a wink and a smile
And return the favor
Burn your fucking name
In every moment you touch

Never use your words
To get someone to love you
Speak your truth
And find out who already does

I know it feels like
You can't change the world
No matter how hard you try
But the world is changing
And every single change
No matter how big
Or how small
Was brought about
By someone just like you
Who cared passionately
And never gave up

No one ever

Won a war

Without losing

A few battles

I'm still standing

This shit ain't over

In the darkest days
It becomes even more
Imperative
That you find
Whatever light
You may possess
And shine it
As brightly as you can
Not just so you can see
But so those around you
Can find their way
As well

Stop living check to check

Live embrace to embrace

And kiss to kiss

Live with a heart that's full

Even if your bank account is not

They're probably not
Going to like you
When you're not
Like them anymore
But when you can
Look at yourself
Without hating
Everything you see
You're probably not going to
Give a fuck

You could
Spare yourself
A great deal
Of angst
If you would
Just learn to
Laugh at yourself

You've worn that mask for so long
Woven together pieces
Of your own defense mechanisms
And other people's expectations
With roots that dig down
Deep into your skull
You know you need to take it off now
Or you will never be happy
It will not be easy
And it will hurt like hell
It will be a violent affair
With fingers digging into skin
Ripping away everything
That you are not
And what remains will be
Terrifyingly raw and honest
Mangled flesh and blood
Hanging from a naked skull
But it will be you
And it will be fucking beautiful

With age comes

The realization that

Some battles

Don't need to be fought

So you can

Save your energy for

The ones that can't

Be avoided

If you want to become
The best version of you
Define yourself
By what you love
Rather than
What you hate

I CAN SMILE

Forged by years of loyal slavery
Conceived in every debt repaid me
Spawned in hope that never saved me
Formed by lies and human fakery

These are the things that made me

But now I've found a place inside
Intrinsic value I once denied
A place of rest from long, hard miles
Like beauty born of something vile

And in this moment...

I can smile.

Turn the page for a special
sneak peek at

The follow-up collection to
THAT'S NOT POETRY

Available now from
Big Small Town Books!

Let that shit go
That's what I do
That's what I've always done
But what do you do
When that shit won't let go of you?
That's when you just have to ride it out
Painful as that ride will be
Feel those feels
Cry those tears
Wrestle with that knot in your stomach
That won't let you sleep at night
Until time finally does
What time always does
And then
Let that shit go

I wish I could sing
but I can't carry a tune
In a backpack
Or hit a note
with a Louisville Slugger
I know
I'm already smart
And handsome
I've got abs and pecs
And an awesome beard
And a big dick
But goddamn
I wish I could sing
Maybe then
I would love me

That moment
After a
Long
Slow
Soft
Kiss
Where you both gasp for air
And you're so close
That your lungs
Are competing
For the same oxygen...

I love that moment

Photo Credit: Natasha Welch

J. WARREN WELCH is a husband, father of daughters, lover of squats and deadlifts, wearer of leggings, commenter on social issues, podcast host, and writer of prose and poetry who resides in East Tennessee.

You can find him on social media at:

 @j.warren.welch

 J. Warren Welch

 @J_Warren_Welch

.

Made in the USA
Middletown, DE
19 October 2020